MMLL
MIKE McCARTNEY'S
LIVERPOOL LIFE

garlic
PRESS

MMLL
MIKE McCARTNEY'S LIVERPOOL LIFE

ISBN 1-904099-06-8 (hardback limited edition)
ISBN 1-904099-07-6 (softback)

Reprographics Plan 4, Spain
Printed and bound in Spain by Bookprint SL

First published in 2003 by
Garlic Press Publishing Ltd
71 Prenton Road West, Prenton,
Birkenhead, CH42 9PZ
Tel: +44 (0)151 608 7006

email: guy@garlicpress.co.uk

www.garlicpress.co.uk

 hank u...

...very much to our main sponsor Nikon
who have made the MMLL project possible.

Dedicated to Ro on 29th May 2003
with MUCH love

oreword

Lord Puttnam of Queensgate CBE

Public libraries aren't all that fashionable nowadays. More's the pity, because they were a brilliant concept that allowed generations of people to navigate a place for themselves in the world. To millions they have offered salvation from the impoverishment of an inadequate education and fuel for their sometimes dormant, but frequently fertile imaginations. I think it's safe to say that thousands, probably hundreds of thousands, owe Britain's library service everything.

Which leads me to wondering whether those responsible for the running of Allerton Library in Liverpool have any idea of their gift to the world – or more precisely, to the documentation of the most colourful period of Liverpool's cultural history? The books on photographic theory and practice that Mike Mac borrowed (never to return) from the library in the late 1950s are the true genesis of this remarkable little book of treasures. Should they care to tot up the accumulated fines (with interest) then I guess the royalties from this book would be gone for a Burton.

I mention my gratitude to libraries in general, and Allerton Library in particular because of my admiration and affection for this book. It's an absolute jewel! It's funny, it's wonderfully unselfconscious, and it's very revealing. Mike has a great eye: he proves it by appreciating the way in which the rapidly disintegrating negative of Philamena in the Jacaranda offers up an image that any number of 'artists' would die for.

Mike sums his own book up beautifully: "The 1960s were five, ten, then 25, and now 40 years' aggro." It's his belief that what was going on at the time was worth capturing that allows people like me to have a window on their own time.

For that, and much else – thanks, Mike.

ntroduction

Welcome to the weird and wonderful world of Mike McCartney.

A black and white world of Liverpool in the 60s, which, like the Wizard of Oz, could spring into rainbow colours at any time, by using your imagination. A unique world, and period in time... of Scaffold(ing), Rock 'n Roll, self portraits, family, Queens, first cameras, first skools, first groups, first cars, etc, and all set in the vibrant, one and only, centre of the universe: Liverpool. Hope to see you in my world, and in the wise, witty words of that seriously silly supergroup Scaffold: 'Thank U Very Much'.

Yours,
Mike McCartney

ex-McGear
ex-Scaffold
ex-actly!

'Here we are, where are we?'

(as Dad would say)

My first photograph!
After borrowing the family Kodak Brownie Box camera to record low flying
seagulls the size of GIANT albatrosses over the back garden of our home,
20 Forthlin Road, Allerton, Liverpool, I took the film to be developed at the local
chemist, resulting in this tiny black smudge above the Police Training College,
which made me think: 'There must be *more* to photography than meets the eye!'
As there were no Bresson, Brandt or Bailey videos on photography in those days, I
got the 86 bus up to Allerton Library, took out all the available books on
photography and set about learning my art.

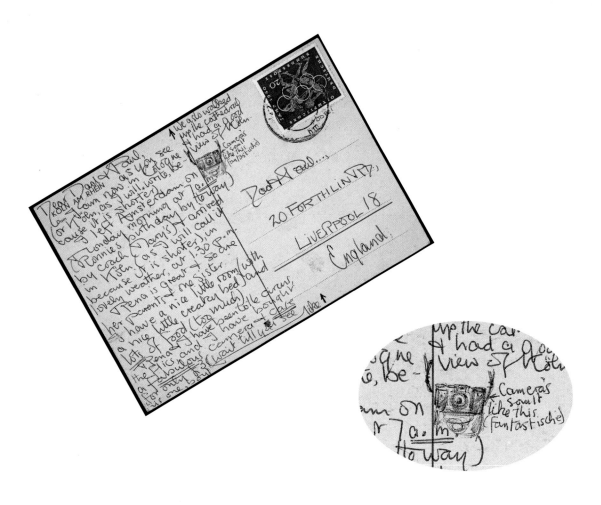

Me and 1st camera, + 1st MJQ album, + octopus!
After reading the books from Allerton Library, it was time to experiment with
photography. Taken on my first Retina 2¼ square pop-out camera bought in Köln,
Germany, on a school exchange trip, this is one of my first self portraits in the
bedroom mirror of 20 Forthlin Road. In the foreground, next to my octopus, is the
RCA album by John Lewis, Percy Heath and Connie Kay... *before* they became the
Modern Jazz Quartet.

Me and 2nd camera

Can't even remember the name of my second 35mm camera (plus viewfinder) but the National Trust of Great Britain would be fascinated with this image, taken in the front parlour mirror of Forthlin Road. When they bought our old home they had great trouble in tracing and buying the 'false brick' wallpaper, which the mirror is hanging on. In the end they gave in, but my wife Ro suggested: 'Why don't they paint it on the wall, from your photograph?' (Over to you, NT)

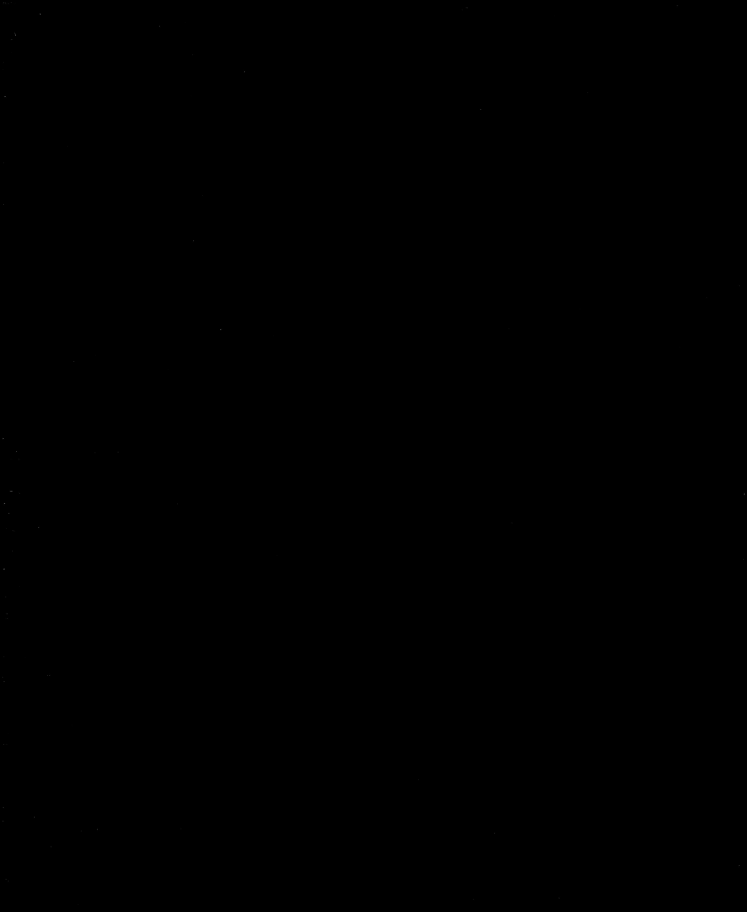

Me and 3rd camera

(overleaf left)

This was in my hairdressing days, ie a clean cut reflex-tive me with Bobby (fan club secretary) Brown, taken by cable release on my Hamburg bought Franke & Heidecke Rollei Magic twin lens reflex camera, in the bedroom mirrors of 20 Forthlin. This was the $2^{1/4}$ square negative camera that got me into printing, but I didn't exactly have the *right* studio conditions. I couldn't afford an enlarger, my 'darkroom' only became a dark room when it became dark outside, and my 'dryer' was a string attached to these mirrors across my bedroom into the wardrobe cupboard, using ladies' hairdressing clips to secure the $2^{1/4}$ square prints, till they dried.

Mad Mick

(overleaf right)

A rather over the top shot of Mad Mick Mac and Rollei Magic practising cable release photography. Again taken in the three-mirrored dressing table of my back bedroom, this time showing my first Phillishave electric razor, plus darkroom accessories of orange tungsten light and black & grey rotating Paterson developing tank.

Me and 4th camera (with 3 eyes)

Taken on my *Thank U Very Much* Nikon camera. It was so named after ringing my elder brother to thank him for his 1966 Christmas present of an expensive Nikon camera (in purple velvet lined leather case); whilst waiting for him to pick up the phone, a ditty popped into my head. When he eventually picked it up, instead of talking, I sang the little ditty... "Thank U very much for the Nikon camera, Thank U very, very, very much". The rest is, as they say in Gayton folklore, history.

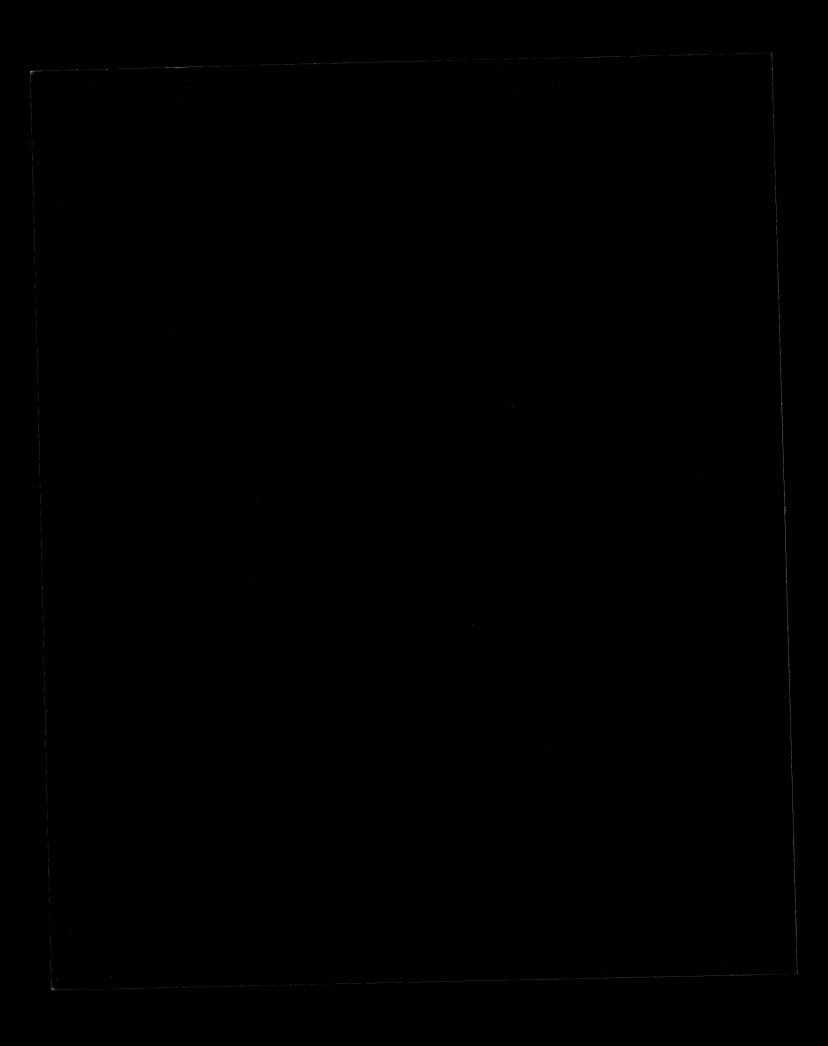

(overleaf)

The Inny

Liverpool people have a notorious habit of abbreviating *anything*, hence when I joined my new city centre school, the Liverpool Institute High School for Boys, it quickly became the 'Inny'. The photograph not only shows the adjoining (black!) Art College (which I desperately wanted to go to) but also the Inny's upper and lower school yards with their Fives courts and toilets for 1,000 boys! Once, when I threw a water bomb from the upper to the lower yard and managed to drown school prefect Peter Sissons (now one of Britain's most famous news readers), my reward was a caning from the head, Mr JR 'the Baz' Edwards.

'Elvis' me posing over Liverpool

Gaining illegal access to the Art School roof, this is schoolboy Mike, hiding my uniform under my brown mac and trying to look like Elvis the Pelvis as much as possible. I would set my camera on its tripod, focus on my schoolfriend Gerry Poole, then swap places so *he* could press the cable release to record *me* for posterity. As backdrop I chose the Inny (plus lower playground) with the back of E Chambré Hardman's house, and a distant Liver Building.

The alternative school photograph

This was *my* version of the official school photograph, which was usually taken in two halves: 500 boys in the lower school and 500 boys in the upper school. Because we were about to leave the Inny, we were allowed to 'goof around a little in school', so this is me and class mates (plus Bin Lidon!) in the upper yard, which adjoined the Art School (where John, Stu, Cyn and Geoff Mohammed were ensconced).

Hope Street (- Cathedral)

Taken just after the 'Elvis me' image from the Art School extension roof, this photograph is of Hope Street, a street of hope which links the Protestant and Catholic Cathedrals. It was many years later, whilst printing up this negative for an exhibition, that I noticed what was missing ... a cathedral!

Hope Street (+ Cathedral)

After discovering Hope Street without its Catholic Cathedral, or 'Paddy's Wigwam' as we call her, I decided to retrace my steps some 40 years later with the same Rollei Magic camera, plus black and white film. This is the result, and to help you Spot the Difference, the trees in Blackburne House yard have 40 years growth, a chimney and church have disappeared, and now there's... a cathedral!

A 'Professional' Lewis Collins (+ bandage)

This was taken in the dispensary of André Bernard's hairdressers in the city centre (now the MacDonalds opposite Lewis's!) and features a young fellow apprentice Lewis 'Bodie & Doyle' Collins. From the dispensary hatch it *appeared* that one of us was pouring beer shampoo (with real beer) for the ladies' hair, but the other one was actually crouching below the hatch with mouth wide open... we never missed a drop. Even at that age he looked good, but would look even better in a leather jacket. Wouldn't you agree, Lew?

Dad on piano

A memory I've had all my life, but this is the only *photograph* of my Dad actually playing the piano. He was in great demand at parties (ie he was the family's mobile disco) and there would always be two or three half pints of beer lined up for him on the top of the piano to keep him going. Here he's talking with his youngest sister Jinny (Mac) in her twin set and pearls, whilst the other partygoers are patiently waiting with their requests.

Dad and dollies

This is a nice change, several years after Mum died, seeing a more relaxed side of Dad, chilling out with two lovely family friends at an Aunty Jin & Uncle Harry party at 147 Dinahs Lane, Huyton, Liverpool. The lady on the right is trying to tell us she might have had ONE too many shandies... As you can see, Dad was always *correctly* dressed, even at a family party.

2 Number 1s

After his 'hard day at the office' (doing the accounts at Dad's cotton firm
A Hanney & Co) and after her 'hard day at the home' (doing our washing, ironing
and cooking when Mum died) Uncle Albert and Aunty Milly, who journeyed across
the River Mersey to help us out every alternate Monday, certainly deserved a
rest. It was only years later that I realised that this sneaked image of Dad's sister
with her husband was of interest, in that both of them were Top of the Pops!
Uncle Albert got to No 1 with our Paul's group Wings, and Aunty Milly (who 'ran
willy nilly') was in Scaffold's No 1 hit, *Lily The Pink*.

(overleaf right)

Nash takes a nap

A relaxing, meditative image of ex-Hollies singer Graham (Crosby, Stills, Young &) Nash on a train from Scotland en route to Liverpool, dreaming of his first Newcastle Brown beer. Gray, Alan Clarke and Scaffold stopped off at Newcastle to sample this as yet unknown strong ale, but before we even got to the pub, we spotted a tiny, one man Make Your Own Record booth on the station platform and couldn't resist squeezing two Hollies and three Scaffold in, to perform Tiny Tim's *Tip Toe Through the Tulips* at full falsetto. John *Tiz Waz* Gorman still has the 'ScaffHolly' floppy disc somewhere.

(overleaf bottom)

Dreaming up poems

This is another sneaked image, this time of Scaffold member and poet Roger McGough, 'resting' on the same train as Graham Nash en route to Liverpool from the east coast of Scotland. I have many fascinating photographs of Roger, but sadly he'll never see them as he lives in London.

(overleaf top)

Alan 'Hollies' Clarke

This image of the lead singer of the Hollies, Alan Clarke (plus friendly Geordie docker behind) completes the sleeping trilogy of Nash, McGough, and Clarke (sounds like a US supergroup or firm of accountants) in somnambulance corner, on the east coast train to slumberland zzzzZZ

(page 40-41)
My first car... a Classic!
Being working class people, born into a vicious class controlled system, with little or no hope of ever breaking out of the poverty in those days, can you begin to imagine what it was like to take delivery of your first car, before you even turned 20... and a Ford Classic too! Hence its proud pose in front of 20 Forthlin Road, the house that the National Trust bought. At first they weren't convinced about buying a tiny home in the middle of a row of terraced houses, as they usually purchased castles, baronial halls and stately homes for the nation, but my photographs of this era (including this one) clinched the deal.

A classic car... head on
Another proud pose in front of 20 Forthlin. The road at the top of the picture is Mather Avenue, where the Queen tried to knock me down. I think it's a Ford Popular which is passing – the typical shape of cars in those days. That's why having a British racing green car with such sleek lines, twin headlights, a back window that went *in*, and small American style fins at the back, was such a coup.

(page 42-43)
Ford Classic through Mum's net curtains
When you've taken pictures of the front, back and sides of your new car, there's only one shot left: from the top. Taken through the net curtains of Mum and Dad's bedroom at 20 Forthlin, this shows the cool going-in back window, plus two lads heading towards the flats at the end of our road. One of them might be Terry Sylvester who, years later, replaced Graham Nash in The Hollies (small world).

A Classic spaceship
A rear view of my Ford Classic (showing the British version of American fins) about to take off from Forthlin Road into the sunset. Note the old fashioned cars of the day in cool contrast to my classy Classic. The flats on the right are where Terry Sylvester lived. What's even stranger, many years later, when Terry had finished with The Hollies, he ended up across the water of Merseyside in the next village road to me.

George's Jag

Being a working class lad and having just bought a gleaming MkII Jaguar to replace his Ford Anglia, it wasn't long before George knocked on our Forthlin Road front door. "Quick, Mike, get your camera and take a picture of me with my new Jag."

"But George, it's getting dark!" I observed.

"Bring your flash" said George.

"And it's started to rain!" said I.

"Bring your umbrella" said George.

A 'strange car' outside the house

It isn't often that a car like the Queen of England's drives up to your home and stops. But when your elder brother joins a successful pop group it happens more and more. Strangely, whenever the old fashioned limo appeared, so did the fans, out of nowhere, clutching pens and paper. Look, they've even nicked our gate...

God bless the speeding Queen

Having missed Her Majesty's Rolls Royce entrance into Liverpool past the top of
Forthlin Road (in the late 1950s), I was determined not to miss her going back to
Liverpool Airport. When I first jumped out of the Mather Avenue tram lane
bushes, I swear the security cops thought I was going to mow Her Maj down, but
when they saw a schoolboy holding the family box camera, they allowed me to
snap this fab pic of the Queen of England, waving regally - to anyone.

Cable release me, 2 bowlers & a light bulb

This is me experimenting with light bulbs in the bedroom of No 20. As you can see I'm taking the photograph by cable release and it must have been taken during daylight, as I've wedged a blanket over the window. My hand painted pelmet is above the blanket and some of my artwork adorns the walls, but please don't ask what I'm doing with two bowler hats: I have no idea. Dad did *not* wear a bowler, he wore a trilby (which *could* be why my son Josh calls his rock 'n roll band... Trilby).

'Jumpin Mick Flash' in borrowed leather jacket

This is a young me (looking like a mixture of my three sons, Josh, Max and Sonny) dressing up for the occasion in big brother's leather jacket (which was borrowed by a professional hairdressing friend, but never returned!), plus black René Magritte bowler hat. Taken in my Forthlin bedroom (with artwork on the walls) this is my first attempt at something the library books called 'bounce flash' on my first Köln pop-out camera. The cheap flash gun was a little too near, and as you can see, I nearly blew my ***** eye out.

Me under chair
Not content with *sitting* for self portraits, I took the mirror off its hinges, propped it up against the chair and lay on the floor for this one! To the left you can see a bottle of developer, jug and fixer tray, and in the back ground, an *Operation BIG BEAT, Tower Ballroom, New Brighton* poster for Friday 10th November 1961. This very poster was recently on sale at a Christie's auction for an incredible £4,000-£6,000 (Should have kept it).

Me times three, + Peggy Lee

More light experimentation in my bedroom, this time using three mirrors and angling them to get me and three Scaffold nooses in shot (I must have just started with my group). Carefully arranged round the bottom of the image are family portraits, a *House At Pooh Corner* book, the *Peggy Lee & George Shearing* and *Ray Charles In Person* LPs plus - wait for it - my octopus.

Me in glasses with octopus head (or 1st blond dreadlocks)
The more interesting aspect of this rather out of focus image (taken on my
hand-held first camera) is the bedroom wall/artroom. Immediately behind my
rasta locks, is the one (and only) prize I got at High School. Realising that an
academic career was not in the offing at the Inny (as the only thing I excelled at
was art) I was now heavily into Surrealism and Salvador Dali. So, knowing my
entrance for the school's big Hobbies Day Exhibition stood *no* chance, I had
nothing to lose by sending in this painting of my profile in a red white and blue
sky, plus army boots and *one* finger protruding through the carpet! Strangely Mr
(Stan) Reed gave me first prize. I sometimes wonder what became of it.

(overleaf, left)

The Shadows

When we were young, one of the most successful groups in the country was Cliff Richard & the Shadows, so you can imagine the surprise and one-upmanship when Paul had his big 21st party at Aunty Jin's house in Huyton, and... the SHADOWS turned up! (*Our kid's group must have been getting big.*) In a rather dark room are Dad, Aunty Jin and the Shads.

Hank

Although the Shadows were a more respectable, mohair suited, showbiz group than heavy, grunting rock 'n roll, when they appeared at the 21st party we at least had the chance of passing Hank B Marvin and whispering: 'Hi, Hank'. Here he is with cousin Di and Dad. This was the party where John famously belted Bob Wooler; but just before that, aled out of his head, John stood about a foot away from me and Gorman as we tried to perform a Scaffold comedy sketch, repeating loudly, over and over: 'Thass not funny.' (I blame Roger's script.)

(overleaf, right)

Liverpool party

One of our favourite Liverpool groups was The Fourmost because they tended to be less serious than the rest. This lightbulb top-lit image was taken during Paul's 21st party at Aunty Jin's home in Dinahs Lane. This image is Billy '4most' Hatton enticing John Gorman and George (to name but two) on to the dance floor.

Dressing up down the Cavern

Because the Fourmost were more comedic (ie had a laf on stage) they were one of the few groups that my brother and his chums mixed with on stage. This image was taken from the back of the Cavern by the entrance steps at a Christmas do with Mike (4most) Millwall borrowing George's jacket, Brian (4most) O'Hara borrowing a violin and his mother's scarf, and George borrowing a dressing gown and someone's Christmas cracker hat. I've just realised, sadly, none of these young men are now with us.

Passing muzos: Jeff Beck on geet

In nineteen hundred and frozen to death, Scaffold were the comedy comperes on a rock 'n roll tour with Manfred Mann, The Yardbirds, Charlie & Inez Fox, Paul and Barry Ryan, Garry Farr & The T-Bones, The Mark Leemon(ade) Five, to name but one. This is a stage photograph of a young Jeff Beck (who had replaced Eric Clapton on guitar) with the Yardbirds. Jeff was one of the first guitarists I'd ever seen to experiment with the feedback of his guitar on the amps. The out of focus singer in the background is Yardies lead singer Keith Relf (also no longer with us).

Passing muzos: The Flowering Hollies
Scaffold and I were providing the light relief on a Hollies/Paul Jones tour. My 'Tommy Cooper' trick flowers had gone missing during the tour, but one evening they magically turned up in the middle of the Hollies act. This is Graham Nash (before Terry Sylvester nicked his job) trying to figure out exactly where my flowers had appeared from.

1960s Liverpool skyline

Because of the pollution and smog in those days, most of the buildings in Liverpool were black. This is a tramp and a drunk and a German girl in the gardens of St George's Hall, city centre. To the right is the entrance of the Queensway Mersey Tunnel (plus Hessys music store) and in the distance you can just make out the birds on top of the Liver Building, but this view today, from the same place, is totally unrecognisable.

Adrian (Ade) Henri

When fellow André Bernard's hairdresser Mike Weinblatt introduced me to John Gorman, Roger McGough, Celia Mortimer, Jenny Beattie and artist-poet Adrian Henri at the Hope Hall (now the Everyman Theatre), we all performed under the name of The Liverpool One Fat Lady All Electric Show (don't ask me why) but at least Scaffold evolved from this rather Pythonesque title. A lovely, bubbling man, this is Ade, plus Marvel comic, with first wife Joyce (both, as Ade would say, now pushing up the daffodils) in front of an original Henri painting.

A hedgey Scaffold

Three 'lively wacker wits' (as the media described us) in our back garden hedge. As you can see, we could easily be mistaken for a heavy metal punk group and indeed we would have been the biggest rock 'n roll band in the WORLD, only for the fact that we couldn't play instruments or sing. So we settled for being a nice, friendly, poetic humour group instead. As nobody could pronounce our Liverpool One Fat Lady All Electric Show name, we thumbed through Roget's Thesaurus and out tumbled... SCAFFOLD (into a hedge).

Scaffold on bomb site

(overleaf, left)

This is Scaffold in more sombre mood, with John Gorman's nose predating *Clockwork Orange* and *Slipknot* by years. Just prior to this we all had safe, respectable jobs for life, with John as a Post Office engineer, Roger an English teacher and me a ladies' hairdresser, but when Mersey Beat came along and they needed a contrast to all the pop groups, they offered us a five minute comedy slot on local television and we all jacked in our jobs immediately.

Gorman on steps

(overleaf, right)

There are so many Gormo stories but for starters... after John had got Cathy *Ready Steady Go* McGowen to open his *Through The Looking Glass* boutique in Liverpool, the next door hairdressing shop (owned by ex-André Bernard stylist Mike Weinblatt and old friend Roger 'CT' Cliffe-Thompson) noticed a DRAMATIC increase in their electricity bill. At first they put it down to all their hairdryers, but eventually discovered that John had plugged in all his dressmaking machines into *their* meter, thus trebling their bill...

Pop group Scaffold: serious pose

(page 78)

After reading all the photographic books and having practised on myself, relatives, cars (and seagulls!), it was no great effort to set up my camera in Gormo's 88 Rodney Street Liverpool flat, to record for posterity the sexiest pop group in Great Britain. As we had to learn how to pose, and as I wanted to show *both* halves of Scaffold, the first image had to be 'serious'. We all did very well, particularly me, until I got the prints back and noticed the big boil on my nose.

Pop Group Scaffold: smile pose

(page 79)

To show the *other* half of Scaffold's new showbiz life, I suggested a little lighter mood might be in order, ie a 'smile'; but not just *any* smile. It must be a Sincere Smile. Gorman, in the middle, got it right. We are merely apprentices to the master (NB: McGough must have felt confident – he sneaked his glasses on for this one).

(overleaf, left)
Celia + Dad's apple tree
My turn to snap pensive Celia in our rather overgrown Forthlin back garden. As the shed in the background was taller than the hedge, we would all climb on top for a free Police Horse Show every year. As Celia was at the Art College and the students were always into the *next* phase of everything, she was the one who introduced me to the first Modern Jazz Quartet and Bob Dylan albums (and therein lies a story or two).

Me + Dad's apple tree
Experimenting with my new Rollei Magic camera in the back garden of 20 Forthlin, I got my friend Celia to press the cable release to capture this 20 year old me in woolly jumper, button-down shirt and wooden Scholl sandals, looking magnificent. (I can hear *Frasier*'s Niles saying: "Up Mount Ego, Michael?") Behind the hedge was Mather Avenue Police Training College where they would train dogs and horses by firing guns at them (blanks, I hope), and where my wife's Uncle Frank trained to be a cop, ending up a Detective Inspector in the Liverpool Police Force, no less.

(overleaf, right)
Happy Dad
Being the former Secretary of the Speke Horticultural Society, it was no problem getting Dad to pose in the middle of his prized apple tree in our back garden on a nice summer's day. More of a problem was getting a smile. After Mum died, life wasn't easy for Dad bringing up two teenage sons on his own, so I must have done something pretty impressive (or very silly) to get this lovely, relaxed feeling of a happy Dad.

Mum and her clock

When she was a young nurse and got into debt, Mum borrowed money from her colleague under the *strict* conditions that her friend would 'hold on to her grand-mother clock' until Mum repaid the debt. Sadly Mum died before this could be accomplished, so her friend just kept the clock over the years, but eventually it returned to our family, via her friend's daughter Lizzie-Ann. When we'd finished the prints for this book, my printer pointed out that there were no photographs of Mum in it. I explained that I was only 12 when Mum died, so had no time to take a photograph of her, but then remembered that I'd taken this one of Mum's nurse photo, resting against her own clock. I eventually found the neg, and here (thank God) she is, a much missed Mum.

Jazz band at the Tower

I'd worked my way round the rear of the Tower Ballroom, New Brighton (on the Mersey) and emerged on the back of the stage where (and to this day I don't know why) I took this photograph of a JAZZ BAND (jazz bands were our sworn enemy!). I could understand if there'd been some good looking girls in the audience, but they are mostly men, and bored men at that. I still don't know the name of the band (Chris Barber and Monty Sunshine are the only ones that brother and I can come up with). Any ideas? (PS Long John Baldry suggests Terry Lightfoot.)

'Great Balls of... Jerry Lee' (Lewis)

Taken at the Tower Ballroom and in the early 1960s (Paddy Delaney, the Cavern bouncer, is behind Jerry's knuckles) I gave this photograph to Jerry Lee at a Birmingham (England) concert in the 1990s. He thanked me and said that it was good to have a record of him *singing* in the 1960s, as he didn't remember much of that era (too much 'enjoyment'?)

"You're not actually *singing*" I said.

"Pardon me?" asked Jerry.

I explained that during his concert, all the excited fans had invaded the stage (including me and camera) and he was in fact shouting: "Get these f****** kids off the stage, or I ain't goin ON!" (*click*)

Jerry Lee and Big Three

Again taken in the Tower Ballroom, New Brighton, but this time I was relegated to the audience. As my Rollei Magic was a twin lens reflex camera with the image taken through the *bottom* lens, large crowds did *not* suit this photographic process. The only chance I had of getting anything was to hold the camera, plus flash, above my head and pray. The drummer (on Big 3 kit) and guitarist backing 'the Killer' must be session men (or The Echoes?), because they're *not* the Big Three.

The Big (3) Three

Certain groups in 1960s Liverpool slowly became 'the groups' groups' ie the groups which the *groups* enjoyed, or bothered to watch. Along with the Silver Beetles, King Size Taylor & the Dominoes, The Fourmost and obviously the hip hop death metal Scaffold, for *me* the Big Three... Johnny 'Hutch' Hutchinson drums, John Gustafson bass (who went on to Roxy Music etc) and Adrian Barber guitar... also joined this hallowed in-crowd.

Joe Brown on the Tower

Cockney singing star Joe Brown, with his horseshoe-strap guitar and backing group The Bruvvers (pronounced 'Bravvers' in London) taken from the back of New Brighton Tower stage. Although only part of the *support* act that night, later on in life, George Harrison became such good friends with Joe and his family that he was best man at their wedding (possibly because Joe's wife was one of the Vernons Girls from Liverpool, but *probably* because they were both fans of music hall star George Formby).

The 'Dakotas'

Taken from the balcony of the Tower Ballroom where I earned the nickname
Flash Harry, this is *obviously* The Dakotas. My brother and chums were usually
support to Little Richard, Jerry Lee etc at this stage in their career, so would
have finished their set and been in the van ready to set off, whilst I would be in
the audience snapping the other acts. 'Where's Mike?' my brother would ask.
Brian Epstein and assistant would then go up to the balcony and wait for my flash
to go off in the darkness below. 'There's Flash Harry,' Brian would say. 'Throw
him in the van.'

(overleaf right)

Bruce Channel on the Tower

Shot from the side of the Tower stage, this is a clean cut Bruce Channel* (who looked more like one of my ladies' hairdressing stylists than a rock 'n roll animal) performing the original *Hey Baby* hit, with the distinctive harmonica (or gob iron) help of Delbert McLinton, under the lofty balconies of the ballroom. The balconies were some 30ft high over the dance floor, and if the bouncers had any trouble at the door or in the audience (and to get the message over that they were serious) they would simply take the usually drunk troublemakers up to the balcony and... throw them off.

* pronounced 'Chanel'

(overleaf left)

Bruce Channel: face off

Some times the flash on my Rollei would fail to go off, but with the assistance of the bright Tower Ballroom stage lights you would often get this magnificent, surreal 'face off' effect.

Striped Shirts

When we wuz young, one our big 1960s influences was the satirical TV programme *That Was The Week That Was* (TW3) with a young David Frost. We even left the pub *early* at weekends to watch it on the telly... a *high* honour. David Frost used to wear black and white striped shirts (well, they were on *our* black and white telly!). When our kid started to go down to London, these shirts eventually worked their way back to Liverpool and we started to wear them. What we didn't realise is that we weren't the *only* ones to be influenced by the stripes. (See *Gene Vincent on Cave*)

(overleaf)

Little Richard's back

As it was 2001, I thought it was time to give my 1960s prints a new lease of life, so I took up an offer from Curwen Press (which works with the Royal Academy) to be the first photographer to try out a brand new, lithographic, continuous tone printing process (which they had invented). The first ones were *Me in mirror* and *Ro sew* but then we produced two rock 'n roll versions, for all you rockers out there. This lithograph image, *Little Richard's Back!*, was taken at the Tower Ballroom. It came about after I set up my camera behind Richard, and asked for a little help from Ringo. He misheard my instructions to press the cable release, so when I said: 'Now!'

He replied: 'What?'

'NOW!' said I (too late). Hence Little Richard's *back*!

Gene Vincent live on the Cavern

The second of the experimental limited edition lithographs. I haven't seen *another* photograph of Gene Vincent on the Cavern stage, so this image must be quite historic. Taken from the back of the stage, where only Bob Wooler, the groups (and brothers) were allowed. Around the corner, checking in Gene's black leather overcoat was Cilla Black (and White!) Gene's in cool head-to-toe leathers, singing *Be Bop a Lula*, but you can clearly see that the fans weren't *over* excited by the presence of one of our heroes, as they were waiting for my brother and his group   to come on... particularly the ones in striped shirts.

Freddie 'super' Starr at the Tower (plus mate)
(above)
Like Rory Storm, when he wasn't performing, Freddie had a charming sttutter
when he spoke; but unlike Rory, Fred had a very testing, anarchic, unpredictable
sense of humour. Like John (Lennon) you never knew what they were going to do
next. They were therefore always a tad dangerous and always a *must* to watch.
The things Freddie Starr would put on a plate would make your hair curl!

A 'shaky' Little Richard
(right)
The flash not going off again, gave this shaky ghost-like image of possibly the
greatest rock 'n roll singer of all time. Live on the New Brighton Tower Ballroom,
helped by London based band Sounds Incorporated (plus brass!), this is Little
Richard (Perreman) belting out one of his *Tutti Frutti* rock 'n roll classics to a
lucky Liverpool audience

(overleaf)

Me on the Mersey

I set up my Rollei camera at the top of these Albert Dock steps, on the bank of the River Mersey, and asked my German friend Ursula to press the cable release. I like the out of focus chain right across the middle of the image, and in the background is not only a Ferry Cross the Mersey (when smoke was allowed to pollute Merseyside) but in the very distance is the enormous outline of the Tower Ballroom. When the ballroom *originally* had a tower, it was taller than Blackpool Tower and even the Eiffel Tower, Paris!

Ursula on the Mersey

My turn to take a portrait of my chum from Düsseldorf, Deutschland (plus ballroom shoes). In the background is the Pier Head with a *black* Liver Building (all cleaned up now), a Mersey ferry and distant Tower Ballroom New Brighton (where I spent many happy hours as a child on the beach). After this shot I fell into the River Mersey but, as you can see, Ursula kindly threw in a life belt to save me.

Miller on Merseyside with McCullin

In the mid 1960s Jonathan *Beyond the Fringe* Miller (MD) was commissioned by a prestigious American magazine to write an article on the 'real' Liverpool. He brought with him the famous war photographer Don McCullin, who is seen here changing the lens of his Pentax camera (NB *string* strap!) outside John Gorman's 88 Rodney Street flat. It's a good job Jonathan was a doctor because, after a disastrous attempt to show them the fab, swingin, 'real' Liverpool (where every-thing was closed) he ended up administering to an accident victim who'd been thrown through the window of his Mini, on the outskirts of the *real* Liverpool.

Passing muzos: The Searchers

Waiting for the cameras to record a TV programme for America, this is Liverpool group The Searchers (looking for needles and pinzas?). Their drummer Chris Curtis once stopped me in Liverpool to complain that too many girl admirers were coming up to him and asking: 'Hey, la, are yous Mike McGear from The Scaffolds?' (NB: we have the same Roman nose). 'That's funny,' I lied, 'They come up to me all the time, asking "Are yous a Searcher?"'

Passing muzos: Wayne Fontana & The Mind Benders

On the same telly show, this is a happy Wayne Fontana, plus tambourine. I'd forgotten that the guitarist next to him was Eric (*I'm Not In Love*) Stewart. Later on Eric and I became friends when he joined 10cc and I recorded my *Woman* and *McGear* albums at their Strawberry Studios in Stockport near Manchester. Unfortunately I've not met Wayne (a nice man) since.

(overleaf right)

Passing muzos: Georgie & Eppy

Taken at the same TV studios, this is the moment Brian 'Eppy' Epstein walked straight across Georgie Fame & The Blue Flames' camera shot. Whilst working on this print in the darkroom of my printer's house in Leigh (on the East Lancs road to Liverpool), I mentioned that Georgie used to live in Leigh under his original name of Clive Powell.

'Georgie Fame lived here in Leigh? I never knew that!' said Reiki Ray.

'You do now,' said I.

(overleaf left)

Georgie & Speedy

When Brian had cleared shot, we get sight of an important part of Georgie's Blue Flames... the inimitable Speedy, giving special conga support on one of my favourite GF & the BF's hits... Yeah Yeah!

Eppy on telly

(overleaf, right)

One of the main lessons I learned from the Allerton Library photographic books was 'to experiment' (ie to me, try *anything*). There can't be many mad young men who would draw the curtains of their front parlour, mount their camera and cable release, wait for their brother and chums to come on the black & white TV and then experiment live with different speeds and apertures, until they got a decent picture. Lots of the fab pics had thick black lines across the screen, wiping everybody out. But at least this one of Brian Epstein being interviewed on Granada TV's *Scene at 6:30* survived.

Eppy & Diddy on telly

(overleaf, left)

More television shots from our blacked-out Forthlin front parlour, this time of Brian 'Eppy' Epstein being interviewed by 'Diddy' David (Pilditch) Hamilton on ABC TV: Gerry & the Pacemakers' first ever television show. David was unaware that this picture had ever been taken, till I presented it to him live on the Esther Rantzen TV show in 2002 with Nicholas Parsons, Celia Hammond, Lance Percival, Molly Parkin and Marty Wilde all extolling the virtues of the fab gear Swingin Sixties.

Passing muzos: Billy J Kramer

One of Brian Epstein's NEMS stable, Billy J Kramer, waiting to sing on the telly (hoping the tree doesn't fall on him). NEMS originally stood for North End Music Stores, which was owned by Brian's Dad Harry Epstein. It stood at the bottom of Everton Brow, Liverpool; and being an Evertonian it was from *Harry's* shop that my Dad bought his first piano, on which he would practise (self taught) for his own Jim Mac's Band (small world, ain't it?).

(overleaf)

Me in the Eagle Hotel

Taken in the octagonal window at the top of Uncle Bill's pub in Paradise Street, Liverpool. Uncle Bill was my Mum's youngest brother; when she died we would often visit their home above the pub, where Aunty Dil would cook us delicious Sunday dinners. I had to change my name (to protect the innocent) due to the extraordinary popularity of my brother and his chums; it was at The Eagle where we tried out Mike Dangerfield (from JP Donleavy's *Ginger Man*), and as 'fab gear' were the *in* Liverpool words at the time, it was nearly Mike McFab! We eventually settled on Mike Mc*Gear* as it was the one that sounded most Irish.

Unknown group on the Cave

For the lucky ones who were *there* and actually *played* the Cavern ('poetic word imagery' Scaffold did once... and died a death) the affectionate in-name for the Cavern was 'the Cave'. You can imagine my surprise, some 30 years later when I'm showing some Cavern shots to Chuck Berry in Liverpool (who I never got on camera in the 1960s and who I don't think has even played the Cavern) when he asked: 'Were these photographs taken in the Cave?' Having taken so many images so many years ago, I have no idea who these two rockers are, taken from the back of the Cave. Can *you* tell me?

Celia silhouette

After following the Allerton Library photographic book instructions for years, I started to *bend* some of their strict rules. One of them was never to shoot *into* the light, which I obeyed until I saw Celia's silhouette against the lounge windows of our new house. 'What the hell', I thought and got her to pose with as much light as possible flooding the black leather 1960s furniture, for this award winning shot.

Passing muzos: Elvis in Liverpool

Many people over the years have had the gall to suggest (and even state categorically) that Elvis Presley NEVER came to Great Britain, let alone Liverpool. Well here it is: the irrefutable evidence. Not only did Elvis visit Britain, but here is the great man himself (laughing with John from The Searchers) in the *heart* of Liverpool – a world exclusive, taken by my very own fair hands... Than'youverymuch (uh huh huh).

(overleaf)

Me Mirror

This was the *first* brand new, continuous tone printed lithograph, fresh off the Curwen Press, Cambridge; and is on fine art archival mould-made Somerset paper. This self portrait was taken on my *Thank U Very Much* Nikon camera through an old fashioned mirror in the late 1960s. You can tell it's the Sixties by the hippie carpet and the wooden Dr Scholl sandals with the butterfly painted straps... From a distance, when this image hangs alonside (to the left of) *Ro Sew*, it gives the appearance of eyes, or a pair of goggles.

Ro Sew

Not exactly a *1960s* shot, but I've included this image of my wife Rowena... because she was born in 1960! This was the second lithograph, and features a sneaked photograph of Ro patiently sewing a wedding dress for her sister. It is tradition in her family, that she makes the wedding and bridesmaids' dresses. I was lucky to have recorded the endless hours of sewing that goes into the finished product, which the bride never sees. Equally, the time, patience and experience which Stanley Jones and young Tom of Curwen Press put into these lithographs is a joy to behold. I hope you enjoy them – we do.

Liver Bird beak

The stories and myths surrounding the Liver Birds are almost as strong as 'Did Elvis visit Liverpool?' In 1968 Scaffold recorded the theme tune to the cult comedy TV series *The Liver Birds*, which ran for over 20 years; but the jolly little birds perched on top of the Liver Building are not *all* that they seem. This is a close up of one of the birds, and as you can see, *it actually* looks like a giant, vicious, pop-eyed, alligator-beaked creature, who's just ripped the whisker off a dinosaur, and if the photographer's not careful, his head could be next.

sponsored by Nikon

Cover design: Josh McCartney
Design and typography: Guy Woodland and Arabella McIntyre-Brown
Proofreader: Debbie Woodland

Personal thanks to my old friend David Puttnam,
Elaine (Nikon) Swift, David Fleming & NML friends, son Josh,
photo printers Ray (Reiki) Huey & Reg (Art Skool) Phillips,
Paul (Newz Bar) Flanagan, and Peter (Spud) Grant for introducing Guy and

mike

was born (1944) and brought up in Liverpool • he went to the Liverpool Institute High School, then tried to get into art school but ended up a ladies' hairdresser with Lewis Collins and Jimmy Tarbuck • in 1967 Mike wrote Scaffold's first top 5 chart hit: *Thank U Very Much* (the favourite record of prime minister Harold Wilson) • the next year Scaffold's *Lily the Pink* stayed at No1 in Britain for five weeks, dropped down and went back to No1 (the first record ever to do so) • Scaffold had their own children's BBC TV series *Score with the Scaffold* • Mike's songs introduced decimalisation to Britain and as well as writing music for films, Scaffold did the theme tune to the hugely popular TV series *The Liver Birds*, which ran for 20 years • Mike's first exhibition of photos was in 1985: *Mike Mac's White & Blacks* was shown at the Walker Art Gallery in Liverpool and then in Los Angeles • in 1987 the show went to the prestigious Photographers' Gallery in London, the book *Mike Mac's White & Blacks + One Colour* was published, and the exhibition went to New York • 1988 saw photographic silk screens exhibited in Florida, Washington and New York • an exhibition of new photographs, *Mmm... Mike McCartney's Merseyside*, was shown at the Merseyside Maritime Museum in 1992 with an accompanying book • also in 1992 Friedman Press published *Remember*, a collection of Mike's 1960s photographs in hardback • in 2001 the National Portrait Gallery bought 11 of his black & white images for the permanent collection • he was invited by the Museum of Alberta in Canada to exhibit a new show, *MMLL: Mike McCartney's Liverpool Life* which then opened in Liverpool in May 2003 and has been invited to show at the Smithsonian Institution, Washington DC, in 2004 • Mike has written two children's books: *Roger Bear* (1971) and *Sonny Joe & the Ringdom Rhymes* (1992), as well as his autobiography *Thank U Very Much* (1981) • his talking-visual book *Mike McCartney's Alternative Liverpool* was released on video in 1990 • having worked for the preservation of Liverpool photographer's E Chambré Hardman's house, Mike's photos were the catalyst for the National Trust's restoration of his childhood home, 20 Forthlin Road • Mike has squeezed in many live performances, songs, albums and TV shows with and without Scaffold, including in 1998 *The Gathering at Abbey Road* (where Scaffold recorded their songs) featuring Mike alongside the likes of Fats Waller, Led Zeppelin, Fred Astaire, the Beatles, Glen Miller and Elgar • Mike has six children, is married to Rowena, and has always lived on Merseyside • years in the darkroom have meant Mike now has to wear glasses

Lithographs of
Little Richard's Back
and
Gene Vincent Live on the Cavern
are available in signed and numbered
limited editions of 100
email queries: interfoties@hotmail.com
or contact Garlic Press

Other Garlic Press publications:

Liverpool: the first 1,000 years
Shed KM
The Christmas Day Liverpool Quiz Book
Cross the Mersey (850 years of the Mersey Ferries)
The Grand National Quiz Book

www.garlicpress.co.uk

garlic
PRESS